A Message From Poetsbelief

TRACY CONNOLLY

Published 2021 by Your Book Angel

Copyright © Tracy Connolly

The characters are all mine, any similarities with other fictional or real persons/ places are coincidental.

Printed in the United States

Edited by Keidi Keating

Layout by Rochelle Mensidor

ISBN: 979-8-9850627-1-7

Acknowledgement

I want to pay gratitude to my father who in my life always taught me to be the best I could be. He always steered me in the right direction with the support of always believing in me.

I want to thank my beautiful daughter Emily for her constant praise of all my work. She is the inspiration in my soul to stay writing.

I would like to thank my gorgeous partner Padraig for always being my critique and pushing me to the next level knowing I could do it. He has believed in me since day one.

I would like to thank Keidi Keating my editor and publisher who came and found me on twitter knowing there was something unique about my writing. She has been a great teacher to me throughout my writing journey. I love her spiritual enlightenment, always looking towards the light.

Finally I would like to thank my followers on Facebook, YouTube, Instagram and twitter for their ongoing support in believing in me and encouraging me to write more. Their positivity I will never forget.

Contents

Affected

The fight against alcohol is a battle we will never win.
It's over when they cork the bottle and they've let the
    substance in.
You can call them selfish in everything they do,
But they can't stop the demon arousal, unlike you.

It's sad for the families, the joy it takes away.
There's nothing they can do, only get up another day.
It ruins their kindred spirit, it knocks them on the ground
They've tried so many ways to keep the substance down.

So many people will be affected; it's the climate we endure.
It's not for the faint-hearted; it takes bravery to not be lured.
So if you're reading this poetry, know that I'm by your side.
We must keep the train moving and never let it collide.

I know you keep going back, expecting it to go.
But you must understand, the substance makes you low.
There's lots of better things you could be doing with yourself,
Like leading life's mastership and getting all the help.

Time and time again, you'll hear forgiveness plead its way,
But you must be brave and try to walk away.
There's not much more to say, only to take care of oneself,
And never be alone, always ring a friend.

You must know you are beautiful and totally
    world-equipped.
Believe this all you can, as there is no perfect script.
There's nothing else that matters, your soul must now heal.
Never take for granted: your life is an important deal.

Love the work you
do
because it only
becomes easier
TracyConnolly
19/01/21
Poetsbelief

All Souls Day

With each person passing,
One will need a prayer.
Some will be in purgatory,
Let's show them that we care.

We reach out to the fallen,
Hoping that God will lead the way.
As he shows them eternal light
Surrounding them today.

O Lord, grant eternal rest
To the one's who need you now,
And may they all be forgiven
For the sins that they allowed.

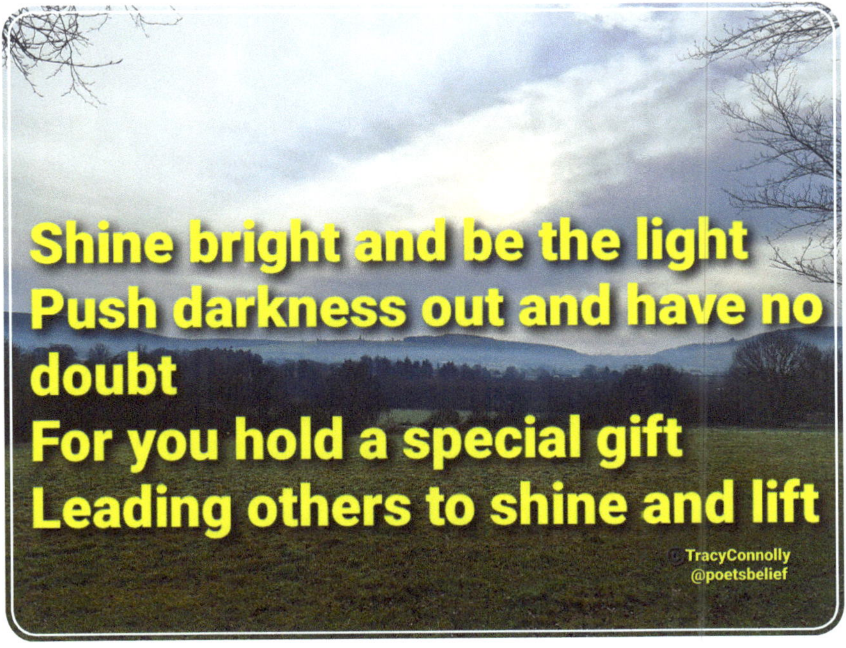
Shine bright and be the light
Push darkness out and have no doubt
For you hold a special gift
Leading others to shine and lift
©TracyConnolly
@poetsbelief

Always in the Dark

You say you have mental illness
And feel always in the dark.
You say you are confused
And find it very hard.

Time is ticking by.
It's not easy to be you.
You try to be your best
In everything you do.

You say you want to live
Much more than you did before,
But the gremlins in your head
Keep knocking at your door.

You know that time moves fast
While fighting demons off,
But you must persevere
And think much better thoughts.

There's days you want to go
But something makes you stay.
It gets harder than before
And the mistakes don't go away.

You try to talk it out
But it seems no one understands
The pain you struggle through.
It's harder to take a stance.

You wonder why you are aware
That life's meaning seems so grey.
You ponder on that thought
And it doesn't go away.

You see others so happy
And you crave that feeling too.
You try to make your mind up
And be happy that you're you.

Your mind loses concentration.
It's harder than it was.
You try to be somewhat normal,
But you are stagnant and so cross.

You've clearly made your mind up.
You're going to do it now,
But when you face the day
You forsake your vow.

The roundabout keeps moving
You're trying to step off
The spin gets somewhat faster
And your thoughts become distraught

You're wanting to get help
But it never seems to come.
You've tried every single avenue;
In your world, many see you wrong.

You know you'll keep on fighting
To prove you're not insane.
You pray you'll see a world
that brings brightness in again.

MISS
T
We have to believe
in life for it is
powerful to our
being
©TracyConnolly02/02/21
@poetsbelief

Auschwitz Hell: Edith Eger

I tried to keep my spirits high,
As I plunged my life into gymnastics.
The scene was set for the Olympic team,
Then crushed for being a Jewish dream.

Transported like a herd of animals
In a filthy cattle wagon tip.
A platform filled with Nazi guards
And prisoners pushed hip to hip.

The angel of death stared on
As the terrified crowd was sanctioned.
A father summoned to the chamber by Nazi guards
A mother I could of saved if I called her sister

My story needs to be heard,
As it's a pain I suffer alone.
A Nazi camp in World War Two
With a hatred of Jews all the way through.

The holocaust rings of German genocide
With local collaborators fuelling.
In a town of Kosice I was innocent,
But anti-Semitism was looming.

So many killings in so many ways
But one strikes deep in my core:
Pesticide pellets with poisonous fumes,
They climbed the walls knowing their dooms.

Being whipped with a dog leash for wanting to pee.
These scenes will always stick in my mind,
But knowing the girl who hit me was suffering,
I forgave her, as my heart was kind.

The murders in camp still haunt me today,
And the words from kapo: "Your mother's burning."
Devastation and pain saturated my heart
As my sister whispered, "The spirit is never apart."

My survivor's guilt lingers strong within
My pain is too much to remember.
The lessons I've learned no one should bear,
As I rebuilt my life while gasping for air.

I know these memories will forever stay,
Like the child that closed her eyes to dance,
Whisking her mind to an opera house in Budapest,
Hoping her life would get a second chance.

We may grow old
But our beauty
Remains deep
©TracyConnolly
08/02/21
@poetsbelief

Be Blessed

Fight for them if you love them.
Start by never giving up.
Their faith is not the same faith,
And their destiny is somewhat mixed up.

Think of them being ill or in distress.
They find it hard to fight the demons that plague.
They're going around in many circles
With a want to escape to their cave.

Look at them and learn to forgive,
No matter how deep your wound.
You are the fortress they cling to,
Without you, their world is ruin.

Think about a master plan you must make.
Let them know you are creating their dream path.
Their vision to themselves is not so clear,
But show them you're trying and you care.

Life is a mystery to us all.
Nobody knows will they win or will they fall?
It's not like a game of cards
Where the winner wins with it's Ace stars.

There's no person who hasn't felt the pain,
Or hasn't been surrounded by demons past,
But some of us are stronger than the others.
We let things go so they don't last.

If we've exhausted every avenue,
It's OK to say that we are done.
We must hand it to the higher person,
And let their faith surround them like the sun.

Life is not that easy for anyone to predict.
It's matters of the heart that hurt us most.
Remember the moment doesn't last forever,
It just fades away like a ball of smoke.

When everything is said and done,
Think about yourself just for a while.
Know that you are beautiful and clever.
And always look onwards with a smile.

Be kinder to yourself and always know,
You are the best that you can be.
Go live your life the way you should,
And be blessed by all you see.

One who creates
Greatness shall live
Forever in the
Making of its stone
©TracyConnolly
10/02/20

Before I Laid Me Down to Sleep

Before I laid me down to sleep,
I thought about my past,
How my childhood memories
Seemed to somewhat last.

As I wandered back in time,
I could see my thoughts aglow,
Trickling in my mind,
Never wanting them to go.

The beauty of that time,
I felt the power in my hands.
While dancing as a child,
In far off distant lands.

Before I laid me down to sleep:
I had started my first job.
It made me feel independent,
Powerful and loved.

Meeting with new friends,
Sharing experiences as we went,
It was all about good timing,
With each day God had sent.

Entertaining with good times,
Shopping that made you gloat,
Fetching a coffee mocha
For sitting and hearing jokes.

Before I laid me down to sleep:
I've aged a little more.
I've had my choice of jobs,
Each one better than before.

The wedding bells rang out,
And families gathered too,
Hoping you'd be happy
In everything you do.

Time goes by way too fast,
Much faster than we think,
For yesterdays become histories,
And definitely make you think.

Before I laid me down to sleep,
I reflect on the day I've had.
All the beauty that surrounds me
And life's treasure, to be glad.

Remembering the news so clear:
Five kilometres our new law.
Thinking it's not so bad,
As the feeling is so raw.

My final thought comes easy,
And I want it so much more.
I close my eyes so tightly,
And dream like I did before.

Angels are protectors sent
from above letting you know
your cared for and loved
©TracyConnolly10/02/21
@poetsbelief

Believe

If you want to get on in life,
Just believe in who you are.
It isn't so very hard to do.
It's up to you to become the star.

No one's going to come along
To show you your true path.
They cannot see your soul,
You alone hide within the mask.

You are the creator of destiny
The one thing you control.
Never let it out of sight,
It's where your dreams unfold

There's a light within your soul.
Only you can turn it on.
So walk out to your goal,
And believe that you are strong.

There are many things you are told:
Not to try or self-expand.
But you know within your heart,
There are dreams to transcend

So believe in who you are.
Don't listen to another's tongue.
Take pride in what you do,
Look up towards the sun.

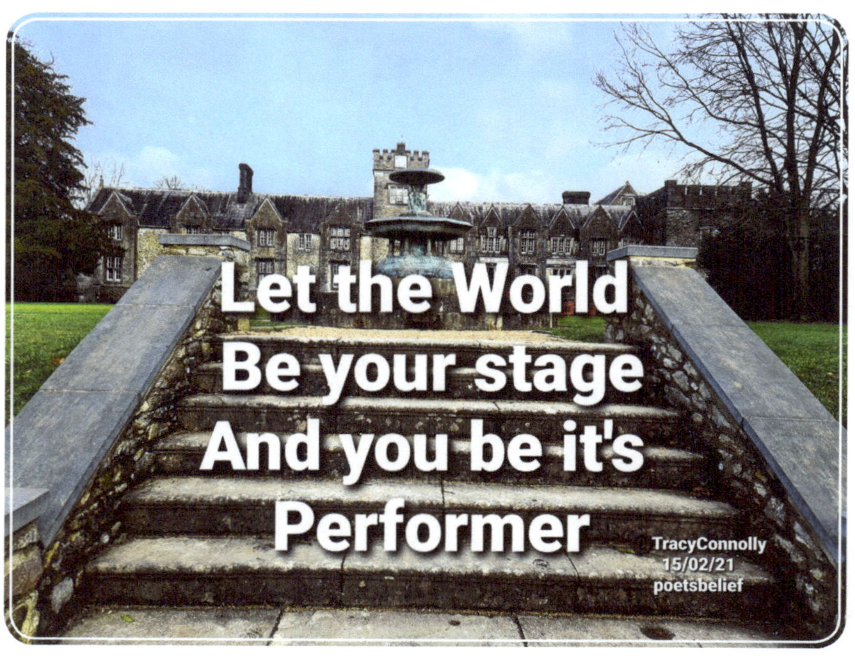
Let the World
Be your stage
And you be it's
Performer
TracyConnolly
15/02/21
poetsbelief

Bounty of Blessings

Christmas aglow with a sparkly feel.
Children's excitement stirs us to heal,
Life somewhat trodden as we plod on our way,
But we must make our mark for Christmas day.

Down from the attic decorations come.
Old Mr Santa sings pa rum pum pum pum.
Candles are lit for that cinnamon perfume.
An atmosphere set as the season now looms.

Neighbours join in with their windows aglow.
The sparkle of lights trickle and flow.
The postman arrives with parcels of cheer,
Spreading the word that Christmas is here.

People shop hard and scurry for deals.
Clogging the aisles, they grab all they feel.
Stockings being filled with new bits and bobs,
And presents being wrapped as if it's a job.

Christmas music played on the radio galore.
With a feeling of gratitude one to explore.
Christmas stockings being hung and the fire ablaze,
The smell of mulled wine feels like happier days.

Coffee shops bustling with people so gay
Gingerbread lattes, all you want on display
Hot chocolate cake with whipped cream delight
Marshmallows with candy cane favours in sight

Turkeys and hampers bought by the load
Ham and spiced beef will never grow old
Breadcrumbs and thyme sold throughout shops
Preparing for stuffing with onions chopped

This Christmas is busy for our longing to be
Our moments are precious and that we now see
We give to the poor and dwell on that thought
For we are OK and not badly off

So now you see there's a bounty of blessings
With so many luxuries given this way
The happiest moments we share with each other
Especially the arrival of Christmas day

Live your life and enjoy
Do not ponder and destroy
Keep your faith as you go
As tomorrow might never show

©TracyConnolly22/09/20
Poetsbelief

Broken

I looked in your eyes and I knew,
You were lost in a world not true.
I felt the pain sever my spine.
A feeling of loss I could not deny.

The anger, the pain, just wouldn't subside.
I felt my heart wrenching like a rough tide.
I couldn't believe you were fading so quick,
As the drug had caught hold, leaving it stick.

It just felt like you didn't care about us.
It was destroying us both, never giving up.
I was overcome with sadness, not believing in you.
It was like being struck by lightning, a terrible feeling too.

Whoever thought we'd be broken just like this?
Our world was in turmoil and it felt heartless.
I'm not writing these words for you to understand,
I'm braving this out so you can make a stand.

The minutes in the car felt like hours,
Until we finally got to the platform stop.
You leapt from the car somewhat sour,
And my body and mind went into shock.

I knew even though we parted I still loved you,
And I think that will always be the case.
No matter where you are, you'll feel it too.
And hopefully someday you'll rise again,
With sunshine on your face.

Don't wait for others
Be kind first
©TracyConnolly13/08/20

Contender

I wake up full of joy.
The day is about to begin.
I see my chest rise and fall.
I breathe out and I breathe in.

The chuckle of a cuckoo bird
Is echoing its voice aloud.
Then suddenly the noise is gone.
A car's engine makes a sound.

I hear some cars travelling fast
To places I'll never know.
I lie in my bed quietly,
Glad of this moment in flow.

What is it all about,
The life that presents me now?
In this raw first moment,
I'm grateful for all allowed.

Silence still awakens my mind.
Life so precious and so kind,
A gift given unto thee.
I thank the Lord, I clearly see.

I rise to this great day,
Its beauty in all its splendour.
For what life has given me now,
I am but a contender.

You are not lost
You just have to find yourself again
©TracyConnolly03/12/12
@poetsbelief

Cork (The Real Capital)

I'm from the rebel County,
Cork City so to speak,
And I've met many a tourist
Who toured our city deep.

They came in all their bus loads,
And loved the Irish so.
They never will forget us,
Don't want to let us go.

The beauty of Cork City
Is magical for all to see,
With Shandon bells that ring out
And tours around the lee.

There's architecture to admire,
With Saint Fin Barre's Cathedral so adorned,
And Fitzgerald's Park with scenic walks
From every corner to be explored.

The Cork Opera House is our theatre
That hosts many an operatic tune,
And dearly loved beside it
Stands Crawford Art Gallery in view.

If you're looking for a soccer game,
Just look for the red and white.
You'll surely hear the screams and roars
The Cork City players will ignite.

The city is enriched in historic remembrance:
Our National Monument designed by artisans
From the Echo boy statue, and Father Mathew loved,
The great Michael Collins, Cork City is your hub.

The English Market's fresh produce beats any, hands down,
Loved by all the tourists who visit our town.
There's a medieval mood you'll get on the Cork streets
And if you visit Cork City gaol, that feeling you will meet.

If you're looking for an interesting bus tour,
The Jameson experience is just the shot.
It was established in the early 17th century.
The visitors' centre is its spot.

Before you leave Cork City,
Visit Blarney Castle to kiss the stone.
They'll say you'll get the 'gift of the gab,'
A gift to bring back home.

There's so many things I could tell you,
But I'll leave the mystery for your trip.
Just go wild on all your fantasies,
As Cork City can't be skipped.

www.tracyconnollyspoetrys.com
@poetsbelief

Positivity is the energy
That our soul needs to feed upon
Without this we are not
A true version of ourselves
©TracyConnolly09/12/12
@poetsbelief

The Critics

People will shut you down,
Shout, "It's not for you!"
Polarize who you are
And pick on what you do.

The simple plan is to ignore
Surroundings of all who hate.
Try to stay right on course
And leave them at the gate.

Throughout your life you will see
Those critics will come and go.
Just stand tall through it all
And learn to let it go.

Be mindful who you pass,
Some have been lured in.
Their wicked ways will play a part
And try to wear you thin.

Don't lower yourself for others.
Never disrespect the things in you.
Think of life as beautiful,
And love everything you do.

Be mindful always of the fact
Your courage outweighs them all.
You're a diamond in the pack—
A friend I'd like to call.

Every experience we've ever had has led us
to exactly where we were meant to be
©TracyConnolly28/11/20
@poetsbelief

DAN

It was just by chance I saw your beauty.
Your happiness resonated to where I sat.
I was amazed and bewildered
To be witnessing a gift like that.

Calmly I did sit,
as I gazed upon an art.
It wasn't any showcase,
Just a feeling from your heart.

The moment was so magical.
I was lucky to have met
A gem within Cork City
Feeding pigeons as his pets.

They flocked from every corner
And some nested upon your hat.
They surrounded you with joy,
As you gave them love back.

Nothing seemed to matter,
As you fed them from your mouth.
They showered you with kisses
As they pulled that bread on out.

I was so intrigued
By you giving them some food,
I asked you for your name.
'It's Dan,' you said aloud.

Now we had made friends,
I wanted to have more:
A picture of this moment,
Captured to adore.

The people would pass by
And mumble that you're great,
And then just walk away,
A time they would erase.

For me, I lingered more,
The joy of it to see,
The birds swooping in and out,
Then sitting on your knee.

Your hand would just go up,
And a pigeon would take land.
You always showed them care.
Your energy did expand.

My time was almost up.
I placed change by your side.
It was a gesture for the birds,
Something I could not hide.

As I turned to walk away,
You smiled at me so much.
I was happy for this day,
And a wonderful human touch.

It is right to do right by others
If they do right by you
©TracyConnolly06/11/20
@poetsbelief

Dementia

You couldn't get the words out.
You tried with all your heart.
You looked at me so sad,
Confused and in the dark.
So I leaned in closer to you,
And whispered in your ear,
'I'm with you, Dad. Here always,
Now and forever, I'll be near.'

We talked about the old times—
Those memories were so clear,
I could see within your eyes.
Your happiness brought a tear.
I always grasped that moment.
You were grateful for our chat.
Somehow it felt like yesterdays,
Telling stories from where you sat.

Then the confusion would set in,
The frustration would be once more.
The pains and aches would follow,
For all of you was sore.
You'd look me in the eye,
Hoping that I'd know
How to take away your pain,
And stop this awful low.

I've always tried new things,
To see which one was right.
You looked on with trust
That it was going to be alright.
I knew it had to be
Something in the room,
So I'd show you many things,
And hope we'd get it soon.

Some days we spent like this,
Others were not so bad.
We'd spend them in the moment,
And try to be somewhat glad.
I know dementia can be hard.
I was so proud of you.
You were the greatest father,
And forever, I'll miss you.

Walk towards the light
Walk away from the dark
Love your soul within
For you it all begins
©Tracyconnolly29/10 /20
@poetsbelief

Forever Heartache

You might have left here,
But this I know:
My forever heartache
Does not go.
You were my dad,
I'm glad to say.
I'll love you always,
Until the end of days.

Words might not mean much to some
But to others they might be the reason to pull through
©TracyConnolly13/11/20

Fungie

In 1983, Fungie arrived in Dingle.
He was a bottlenose dolphin, showing himself off.
Thousands flocked to where he made the bay his home.
Some would live in Dingle for this entertainment alone.

Swimming with the dolphin was magical in a sense.
Some people said Fungie would heal your soul.
He was known to live alone,
But people were drawn to his home.

Fungie brought marine tourism to its greatest height,
Helping pubs, restaurants, and shops stay afloat.
Just an amazing dolphin who generously played.
For anyone who arrived, he'd surely make their day.

The town's lighthouse keeper, Paddy Ferret, as he's known,
Met Fungie at the mouth of Dingle's great home.
He knew it in the water when Fungie was around,
Every ripple that he made–Paddy always knew the sound.

A celebrity dolphin leaping high up in the air,
Always loving the applause and the ongoing cheers.
Many a boat company would give your money back
If you didn't see Fungie doing playful acts.

Then came the news: Fungie had disappeared.
The country was transfixed by his story,
With search and rescue teams already in the seas,
But the days went by and Fungie was never seen.

We didn't know where he came from,
Where he was born in the ocean wide,
But we know he's a major part of Dingle,
Hopefully something we don't have to survive.

The choice was always Fungie's: Should he stay or should he go,
But he chose to remain in the heart of Dingle.
We won't say he's gone, we'll say he's gone asleep.
As we pray to God to mind him in the deep.

Gods little helpers
on the ground will
one day be his
angels he
surrounds

©TracyConnolly
13/12/12
@poetsbelief

Homeless Crisis

My mission here is not to aim the sword,
Or to look upon those who are mistrusting,
But those who know what they do,
Will be reminded on their day of judgement.

I hear a cry for social housing,
And all the people on the waiting list,
Rising rents and unemployment,
People who seek direct provision also hit.

The highest winter mortality rate we have ever seen.
Now fast approaching another winter where we've never been.
Will it have some lasting consequences on their mental health,
From layoffs coming fast and not being able to pay the rent?

Are we to wait on the good Lord's faith
For something our souls now feel an injustice?
To see a person beg, on the ground so cold,
With a society lost and our voice now sold?

Even though people are forever giving,
The law has got to be on our side,
For only they can change these drastic conditions,
And show homelessness a way to subside.

We are living in this small little country
With so many struggling, living in poverty.
Now with a growing problem of homelessness to fear,
We must gather our strength and show them we care.

Why are the hostels being used for some?
When we have the finest builders ever seen!
Surely it's time to take drastic measures
And take a slice out of Ireland's beautiful green.

The Irish are proud and resourceful beings,
But there's hidden homeless in Ireland we aren't seeing.
The wages won't allow them escape from poverty
With the struggling middle class who face snobbery.

We walk the towns and we look around
Only to see wet blankets in a doorway.
A woman sobs as she holds her boy of four,
A deadly sight that we all deplore.

Our community helping with a mug of soup
Cardboard writings: 'Irish and Homeless please help, Thank you!'
Dogs lying loyal to the old man's side.
This country has fallen; please help them stay alive.

If I can touch one life
That's all that matters
©TracyConnolly
20/12/20
@poetsbelief

Human Extract

I watch you sit comfortably.
You stare at a gaze,
You look with great sadness,
To my simple amaze

Pondering what it feels like
For you who sits still,
As words you can't utter
From now and until

You look amazingly beautiful,
Soft and fulfilled.
Nothing can bother you,
As you sit on the sill.

I feel that I know you
Very well at this stage.
You almost feel human.
I'm bewildered to a state.

You leap from a height
And take charge as you go.
Nothing can stop you,
As you swoop to a flow.

You're fluffy and white,
A certain sparkle delight,
With pretty soft paws,
And raccoon hat applause.

You're a treasured personification,
Almost like human extract.
Your beauty is beyond belief,
And incredibly apt

The love that I feel
Is admiration for your soul.
In life you're a joy,
A bond to behold.

I will grieve until I
follow you
then I will be home
TracyConnolly
22/12/20
@poetsbelief

Lebanon

I wondered why it happened.
I don't know why it came.
The attack was horrifying.
Life would never be the same.

A war we never wanted.
Our land should be free,
Free to the people of Lebanon,
We just wanted you to see.

Lebanon, Lebanon, your heart was broken.
I cried a million tears for you back then.
Lebanon, Lebanon, your outcry was so sad.
If I could take back all those teardrops
That you've ever shed…

But came the bloody heartache,
Our lives were torn apart.
We never will forget it.
The war just broke our hearts.

The tension was just brewing
In the fields of the cold war.
I could feel the atmosphere changing,
And hear the screams from afar.

We never saw the outcome.
To be broken just like that,
Our land was so precious,
The beauty just bounced back.

I never will forget you,
The pain that you went through.
You prayed for their forgiveness,
The Lord expected it from you.

Today will be the removal of
I can't
and the rebirth of
I can
©TracyConnolly05/01/01
@poetsbelief

Life from a Fall

Some live a fairytale,
Or so they depict.
I'm happy for them,
If it all fits.

I'm writing this story
About who must know
I've felt the pain
And the permanent low.

So please forgive me
If I don't glow.
You portray your happy,
And that may be so,

But remember the people
Whose days are a load.
For they carry the pain
Not many can hold.

You probably mean well.
You're smiling so bright.
The grass isn't green
On the other's plight.

That's not your fault,
You echo in mind.
Do have some regard
You clearly must find.

Not saying you're wrong
For happiness you hold,
But others are hurting,
And one must be told

Go ride your journey.
It isn't one's fault
I must pick up
My life from a fall.

©TracyConnolly28/06/20

One who creates dreams in a world full of adversity shall flourish in their future
Kingdom
©TracyConnolly08/01/21
@poetsbelief

Love Is Coming

Love will blossom,
Love will come.
It's waiting for you,
Keep it young.

Tell your heartache,
It will be OK.
Tell your mind,
That it's today.

Don't just suffer
Your life away.
Love is coming
Like sunshine rays.

It's up to you
To sing the song.
Love is coming,
Let's keep it strong.

Go find yourself
And ask for it.
Believe it first.
It's sure to fit.

Life is too short
To walk away.
Pick yourself up,
It will be OK.

The past is history.
Today will win.
Take your life back,
And make a grin.

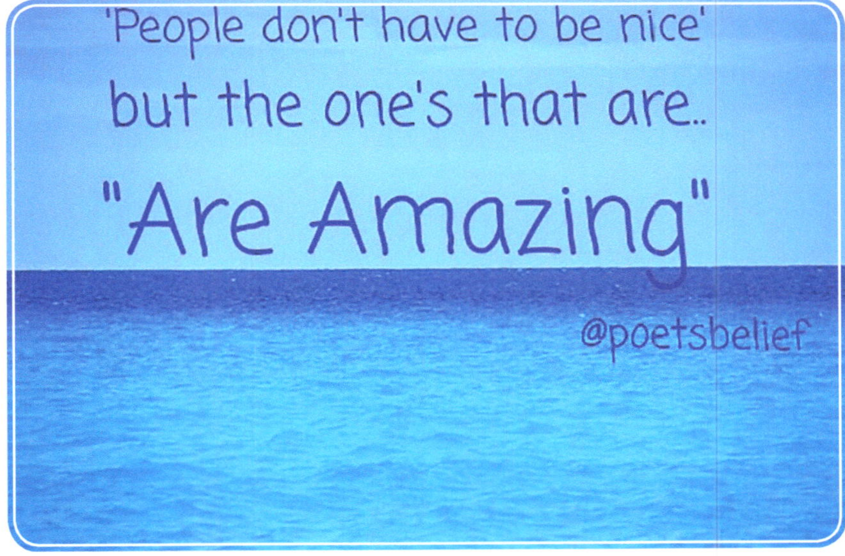
'People don't have to be nice'
but the one's that are..
"Are Amazing"
@poetsbelief

Love Yourself

When things go wrong,
Don't be sad.
You've done your best;
You should be glad.

You can't change people,
Only they can.
It's not your fault.
You're better than.

It's time to breathe
And just let go.
Try be happy,
And not so low.

You've come this far.
You made it through.
See the stars,
And life's pursuit.

Life's a great picture
Only you can paint.
A dash of colour
Would not taint.

So let's be glad
You made it here.
And love yourself,
With no fear.

'People who are afraid
to fail
are not living a true
version of themselves'
TracyConnolly12/01/21
@poetsbelief

Martin's Journey

What does it mean to be homeless?
Can they have a voice that is heard?
Seeing desperation in their eyes, we feel guilty.
A world unimaginable and somewhat blurred.

Anyone homeless I'm sure has a story,
One that hurts deeper than they'd like to tell.
Some may have fallen over drink and drugs,
Others fell apart and some were not well.

So I'm going to tell you a story
About a poor soul who needed some help.
He once was a soldier who travelled
And fell down on his luck himself.

It seemed his life flourished at the beginning
As his family loved army life,
Surrounded by the Curragh plains,
A childhood full of soldiering, squealing in delight.

From father to brothers, he ran a tight ship.
His destiny was army and it's one he would grip.
Combined with a family, he created his own.
With love and romance, his two boys now grown.

Then something happened in the midst of his career,
That shocked and confused him beyond belief and despair.
While fighting the demons, his marriage fell apart.
He could not cope so he broke his own heart.

He suddenly woke up shivering in pain
In an old graveyard, feeling worthless again.
Depressed and worried his new home was here,
He looked around him and shed a great tear.

The struggle was on, he was homeless for sure,
Not knowing his future or what next to explore.
From walking the city by day and by night,
He found refuge in the dead and prayed for the light.

The winter drew near and white blankets did fall,
The escape from bleak conditions was evident above all,
So he dragged himself out and trod on the road,
Presented to a homeless council where luck did unfold.

Spending years in the hostel, he made great friends.
They showed him the way and his nightmare met an end.
He finally got a home to cherish and keep,
Along with The High Hopes Choir, a miracle he reaped.

As we conquer our own
fear
The light radiates from us
Thus drawing people into
the light
we hold a presence
like a beacon shining so
bright
©TracyConnolly16/01
poetsbelief

New Year's Dawning

Love is going to blossom.
Birds are going to sing.
As we celebrate this New Year,
The bells are going to ring.

We thought our lives were over,
As people died along the way.
Now they are in God's arms,
Protected each and every day.

As we move into a new year,
We're stronger than we know.
We've seen the face of terror,
And we're happy to let go.

We know it's not just over.
We must believe there is a way.
And if darkness falls upon us,
We must be strong to face the day.

Life is still a road map
That leads us on our way,
We must be very grateful,
And count our blessings—we're OK.

I want to wish you happiness
In everything you do,
Because from this moment forward,
Your life belongs to you.

Don't ponder on negativity,
And be kind to all you know.
Stay in contact with all your loved ones,
And let your feelings flow.

We cannot change our past.
It's history best left behind.
We've had our true awakening,
And it wasn't very kind.

This year will be so great
As our thoughts design the way.
Let's look forward to our future
And be thankful for another day.

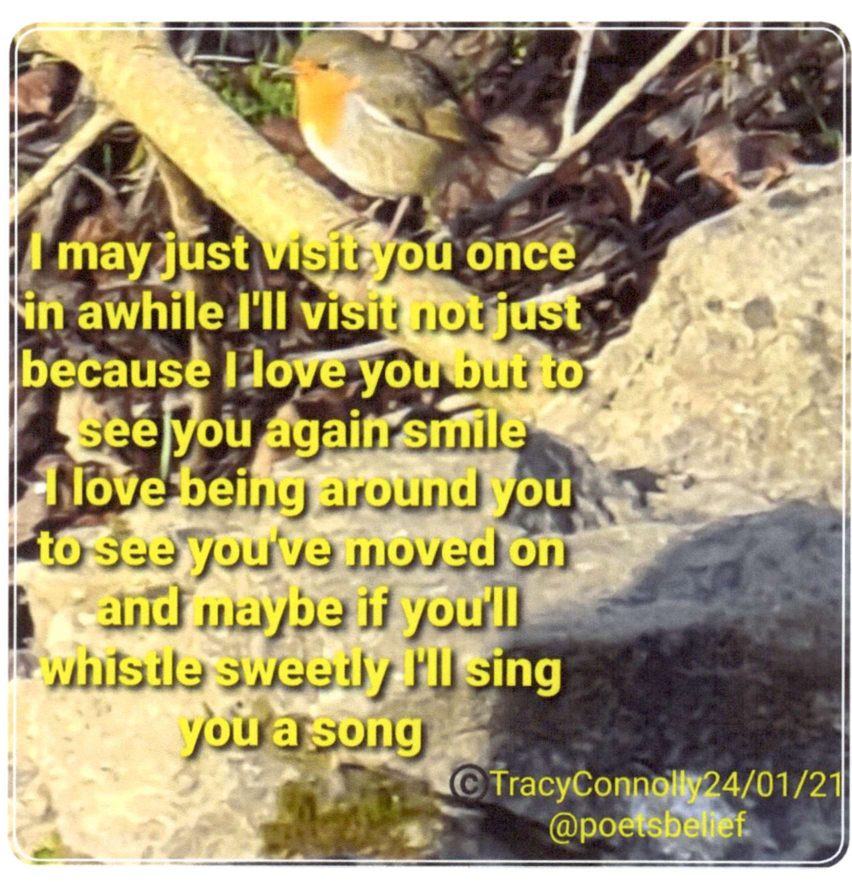
I may just visit you once
in awhile I'll visit not just
because I love you but to
see you again smile
I love being around you
to see you've moved on
and maybe if you'll
whistle sweetly I'll sing
you a song
©TracyConnolly24/01/21
@poetsbelief

Niemba's 9 Lives

We have a memory of Congo past.
It took nine lives of Irish souls.
The sadness we feel will forever last
As Ireland mourned that day so cold.

We know you're in heaven shining down,
Looking upon your comrades in the crowd.
You fought the fight you had to fight.
Now rest easy within the light.

Brave soldiers, you will remain.
On Congo soil, you felt the pain.
Today's a remembrance of your duty done,
And to praise you all as Ireland's sons.

The more we connect
The more we grow
The more we grow the
stronger we become
TracyConnolly01/01/21
@poetsbelief

Nothingness

I never wanted to fall down.
I always wanted to hold on.
It's incredible, I know,
But you were my one.

Do I cry over time wasted?
Do I get angry you're gone?
When I listen to my soul,
I know you belonged.

Then why did it falter?
Who is to blame?
Will I search the world over,
To find nothingness again?

The word 'love' is spoken.
My heart is broken.
I wonder will I heal
From this life that I feel?

I look out my kitchen window,
And the garden seems still.
There's no want from the creatures;
I catch hope in that will.

Do our memories fade away?
Or do we carry them afar?
Let's learn to let love go,
And remember who we are.

This life is very beautiful.
We know that it must work.
Think of a great future,
One that doesn't hurt.

There is always
hope
When you conquer
fear
TracyConnolly05/02/21
Poetsbelief

Pope County Tragedy

Turning on the news was something I'd often do.
Christmas day was here and my excitement grew.
I soon became shocked at what I heard.
Saddened and confused, a tragic story that emerged.

Christmas day tragedy: five family members killed.
Looking at the headline's Arkansas homicide was no thrill.
Deputies dispatched to a residence at 5100 block.
And people at Pine Ridge Road certainly went into shock.

Upon arrival at the residence, the victims were all found dead.
Believed to be family members, the county sheriff said.
Reports were being tweeted, police were outside a home,
Christmas day was over for that family all alone.

As the hours did unfold, more sadness did appear:
Three juveniles and two women we did hear.
Whatever happened in the moment just before their deaths
Will haunt us forever, as they took their last breaths.

For the families left behind
Who ask for help along the way
May the Lord look on them kindly,
And send them help throughout their day.

I want to finish this sad poem
With a thought for you and me,
That even in the darkest days so grey
We must be the light in others for today.

Live your life for today
your worth it in
everyway
live it with peace in
mind
and offer forgiveness
while being kind
©TracyConnolly02/01/21
@poetsbelief

4ᵗʰ Infantry Battalion

Back in 1923 sixty-five battalions came to be,
4th Infantry Battalion became part of the Claremorris
    command.
Several units were disbanded at the end of the civil war,
And 4th Infantry Battalion was formed from the 63rd before.

In 1924, the military posts were occupied by the 4th Battalion
    troops,
Six posts in County Mayo where workhouses became the loop.
Then in 1927, the Battalion transferred to Athlone.
A close relationship was established with An Garda Siochana.

Military parties were called out to search premises and
    make arrests.
The boys on guard in every polling station were an ongoing test.
Protection parties were in order to ensure free speech
    became the norm.
Different ranks marrying Mayo girls, which became the form.

The Battalion's cross-country team won the army
    championships in 1928,
With three individual Irish champs.
Fanning, O'Shea, McDonagh take a bow,
As you gave our Battalion more trophies to be proud.

Few months were spent in Athlone, then Limerick became
   the base.
Before long, 4th Battalion merged into 6th Battalion's home place.
The unit had the highest calibre and was fully trained for war,
But was tasked with cutting turf at Nad Bog as a chore.

From overseas service to IRA border campaign underway,
Aid to civil power is where the 4th Battalion got its name.
Violent outbreak in Northern Ireland was afoot,
And for internal security operations 4th Battalion deployed
   infantry groups.

The Battalion's great efforts were of a certain kind,
With the provision of armed parties always in mind.
From escorts of cash, explosives, and prisoners on the go,
Blasting sites within the state and bomb disposals, they
   would know.

Tom Burke led the army's battalion pipe band
Ahead of the battalion's march from Cork to Bantry in 1942,
And past burglar called Mahony whose last post was renowned,
For many years, no man's funeral was without Mahonys sound.

In 1960, the first unit from 4th Battalion was to serve overseas,
From Kindu to Katanga, no one would believe.
With the terrible Niemba ambushes, every soldier would agree,
That sleeping with their weapon definitely had to be.

We must remember the 450 soldiers of 4th Battalion who
   stood down
Their contribution to Cork and the cause of world peace.
This was a great battalion who simply never strayed.
They won't be forgotten, for in our memory they will stay.

Walk with me
through this life
hold my hand
squeeze it tight
hold me close
within your heart
forever loving
until we part

TracyConnolly09/02/21
@poetsbelief

Second Lockdown

Here we are on the second lockdown,
Thinking that the first lockdown was tough.
None of us could know the outcome,
If this was going to be somewhat rough.

The elderly, vulnerable, single-parent family,
All looking for someone to call,
But now only unless proven essential,
One person can call or none at all.

I hear an elderly person speaking,
'I long for the grandkids to come,'
But now they fear the darker evenings,
And the feeling of loneliness has begun.

Hospital increases with Coronavirus stats.
Property prices rising, I can only smell a rat.
Off, the ballplayers under pressure, cash flow low.
Olympic Games on hold, not knowing when we'll go.

Co Clare produces whiskey with a 21st century twist:
Called "Lock In" whiskey, certain to make you pissed.
People in the countryside posting letters to themselves,
It's come to a certain madness being by ourselves.

Remember we cocooned, always at this time,
With winter fires blazing and sipping our red wine,
Turning on the electric blankets and holding each other tight,
Whispering to each other, 'Things will be alright.'

If they come to pick
Fruit from your tree
As your tree is
plentiful
Always forgive
Never stop giving
© TracyConnolly
08/02/21
@poetsbelief

Stars Align

British Soldiers opened fire on an innocent crowd,
Where a football match became known as bloody Sunday.
Dublin's Croke Park Stadium was a memorable spot,
But dozens were injured and fourteen people were shot.

T'was the guerrilla conflict that began in 1919,
Where British ground forces and IRA were on the scene.
The Irish fought the fight for their independence,
Pushing the British out was just as they meant it.

Three school boys and a bride-to-be
Were just some of the victims who died.
Some ordinary fans who were not well known
Went to the match and never came home.

These were people with families who loved them,
From the boy who climbed a tree so high,
To the woman who was supposed to get married,
And our corner back, Michael Hogan. We cried.

Many years on Tipperary play Cork in the Munster final
In Páirc Uí Caoimh where the atmosphere felt right.
All decked out in their green and white jerseys,
Eighty-five years on Tipp take Cork in their fight.

Tipperary have done it, with history made.
With the colours they wore just the right shade.
For it's one hundred years since the Croke Park event,
And winning that game was a godsend.

Let's pause in memory for the people who died.
Take triumph in the win of a spectacular kind.
Tipperary has now marked history upon the field,
And have honoured the memory of Michael Hogan, now sealed.

The pain of my heartache
does not go
I love you today,
tomorrow, and when I
grow old
your in my thoughts both
night and day
I love you dad
and in my heart you'll stay

Sweet Sixteen

There are moments in life you cherish.
There are moments you'll never forget.
You touched my hands so gently.
Your love swept through my veins without regret.

Your piercing blue eyes stared on me,
Looking somewhat lost in my arms.
But I held you close to my bosom,
A bond that no one could part.

You started to grow up fast.
You made friends wherever you went.
With music and sport you were gifted,
And you triumphed where e'er you were sent.

There were times you'd come to explain
That life wasn't fair to you.
All I could give you was my support,
And tell you that I loved you.

There's nothing I wouldn't do.
You're my daughter, the incredible you.
We flew through the years together,
And you amaze me in all that you do.

Today's very special because it's your day.
A birthday I hope you will never forget.
Sixteen years old and so beautiful.
I'm proud of you and wish you all success.

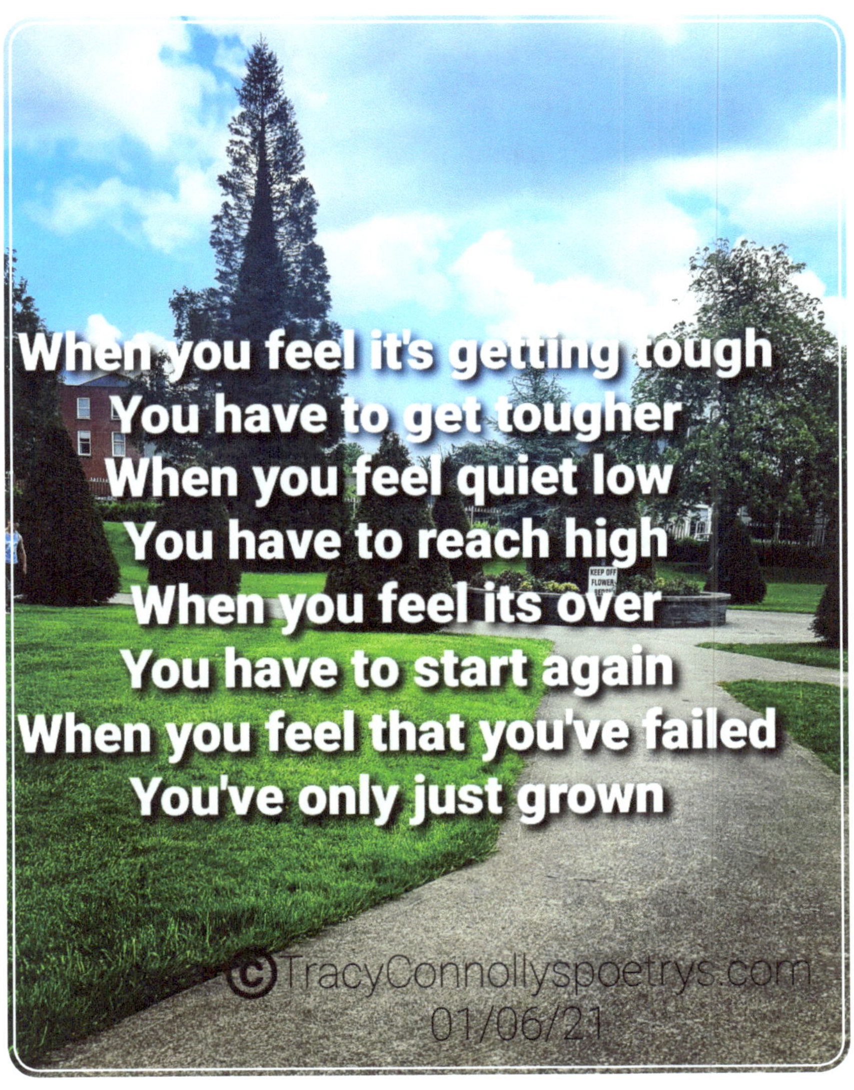
When you feel it's getting tough
You have to get tougher
When you feel quiet low
You have to reach high
When you feel its over
You have to start again
When you feel that you've failed
You've only just grown
©TracyConnollyspoetrys.com
01/06/21

Tears Of Forever

Time is passing so quickly,
I'm wondering what next to do.
Sometimes I fear the moment
Of a life torn without you.

You always filled the room,
Your laughter filled the space.
The smell of your aroma
Somehow hasn't left this place.

I think of a memory fading,
One I just want to keep,
But time doesn't wait for me ever,
And the moment just wants to sleep.

Why did it end so abruptly?
What really happened to us?
I cried the tears of forever;
It was more than just lust.

Where was your longing to be more,
If you thought we were as one?
Was I just a passing thought?
Knowing we'd soon be gone?

What makes two people strong?
What gives them greatness within?
Why didn't we follow that path?
Why did we wear ourselves thin?

It's not about the promised tomorrow,
I know no one can offer that day.
It's about dreams and souls of fire
That blaze and know their way.

We walked many a road together,
We spoke of dreams coming true,
We danced nights under the moonlight,
We sang songs we loved too.

Who knows what you were thinking?
It's hard for me to understand.
This beautiful life is a blessing,
But I feel nothing without your hand.

I have to live a life without you.
It's something I can clearly see,
But know this is not a parting,
For in my mind, you'll forever be.

The Man That I Adore

I never thought I'd love again.
Finding love in the end,
It's a miracle, that I know;
A seed about to grow.

Love is kinder than before.
Love has found me, that's for sure.
The greatest feeling of them all,
A type of love that came to call.

Everything just seems so right,
Like an angel came into my life.
I thought of you in my dreams.
Now you're here, I can but beam.

All my life I wanted you,
You're the man that makes me new.
I couldn't see us two apart.
I loved you from the very start.

You make me feel complete.
The pound in my heartbeat,
The comfort that you give
Makes me want to live.

You're amazing and so true.
I love everything you do.
You're the backbone to my core,
And the man that I adore.

The Substance

'The substance will kill you,' that rings in my head,
But what do you care? You choose it instead.
It's a minefield, I know. Only you can change this,
And your life would be wonderful, streaming with bliss.

Your choice is to run away; it's easier for you
Than to live with the demons your mind puts on you.
Your escape feels like victory, a battle you've won,
But it's a rehearsal of plays you've already begun.

How can you change, what can you do?
There's no easier way than to stop what you do.
You don't care who you hurt, you're troubled for sure.
You can't find the answer or knock on one's door.

It feels like a game, at times you control,
For your moods get colder and insanity unfolds.
It's hard to suppress those moments I endure.
The damage is done and it's the same as before.

The excuses continue as you lie your way out,
Using people around you to cover my doubt.
The more this goes on, the pain just gets worse.
As you trouble my soul, it feels like a curse.

So where do I go and what do I do?
My prayers are unanswered and that's nothing new.
I feel like you're dying. It's crazy, I know,
But what's there for me? Only a permanent low.

I struggle with reality, that it's you I picked,
And the damming of this river is forever adrift.
Your rogue behavior doesn't help in this fight.
It just damages my core and gives me no light.

The change is coming, of that I am sure.
I've dealt with the dramas one can deplore.
I'm not giving up, but this you must know.
This can't go on or I'll have to let go.

When I'm Alone

Oh the days feel long
Without you here.
I never imagined
Those feelings of fear.

Daddy, when I was small,
You carried me around.
People used comment,
'She's taken him now.'

And the night will come,
And the night will go,
But where will my heart beat
When I'm alone?

You were always so kind,
A man I adored.
No one could match you.
No one else I'd look toward.

I never thought you'd go.
How was I to know
One day you'd be gone?
Life would just plateau.

And the night will come,
And the night will go,
But where will my heart beat
When I'm alone?

I sit here in thought.
That's how it goes.
Life's just a moment
That passes in flow.

But if I could get back time,
Just one more day,
I'd be so happy,
And sunshine would stay.

And the night will come,
And the night will go,
But where will my heart beat
When I'm alone?

About the Author

I was a soldier for 23 years and there are two war heroes on either side of my family. They have been decorated with distinguished service medals from the Congo. Most of my family were in the army. I've been in the war called Operation Grapes Of Wrath in 1996 in Lebanon. Its something that will haunt me forever. I've also been to war-torn Kosovo in 2001. I was proud to be a United Nations Peacekeeper because I love to help others. I'm now a retired Veteran. I work part-time in the hospitals but I am mainly focused these days on writing and singing. This is where my heart lives.

I started writing at the beginning of lockdown and it was a very positive journey for me. I found a way to help others through my poetry in unforeseen times. My first book 'Poetsbelief On Lockdown' was published in December 2020 and it feels great now to be publishing my second book 'A Message From Poetsbelief.' I'd like to think that with my poetry anything can evolve. I've been published in many newspapers across Ireland. Today, some of my poems have transformed into song and I'm working towards my debut album. My recent single was released in July 2021, called 'When I'm Alone,' which I wrote after my father's passing from dementia. I have written and composed all of my songs. I love to write and I love the people who I connect with. They are my newfound family.

You can find some of my poetry and videos on Facebook under this link below: https://www.facebook.com/tracyconnollys.poetrys

I'm also on twitter @poetsbelief, Instagram poetsbelief, and youtube Tracy Connolly.